Artists Through the Ages

J.M.W. Turner

Alix Wood

WINDMILL BOOKS

New York

Published in 2015 by **Windmill Books**, An Imprint of Rosen Publishing
29 East 21st Street, New York, NY 10010

Editor for Alix Wood Books: Eloise Macgregor
Designer: Alix Wood

Photo Credits: Cover, 1, 4 top, 7, 8, 12 © Tate Britain; 3, 26 © Shutterstock; 4 bottom,
5 © public domain; 9 top © nga/Rosenwald Collection; 9 bottom © Turner Contemporary,
Margate; 6 © Indianapolis Museum of Art; 10, 11, 27 © Yale Center for British Art;
12-13 © nga/Widener Collection; 14, 15, 16-17, 18-19 © National Gallery, London;
20-21 © John Paul Getty Museum; 22 © Metropolitan Museum of Art, New York;
23 © The Fuller Foundation; 24 © Cleveland Museum of Art; 25 top © nga/Timken
Collection; 25 bottom © Jialing Gao; 28 © Sheffield Museum; 29 © Tokyo Fuji Art Museum

Library of Congress Cataloging-in-Publication Data

Wood, Alix.
J.M.W. Turner / Alix Wood.
   pages cm. — (Artists through the ages)
 Includes index.
ISBN 978-1-4777-5402-3 (pbk.)
ISBN 978-1-4777-5403-0 (6 pack)
ISBN 978-1-4777-5401-6 (library binding)
1. Turner, J. M. W. (Joseph Mallord William), 1775-1851—Juvenile literature.
2. Artists—England—Biography—Juvenile literature. I. Title.
 N6797.T88W66 2015
 759.2—dc23
 [B]
                           2014028091

Manufactured in the United States of America

CPSIA Compliance Information: Batch #CW15WM: For Further Information contact Windmill Books, New York, New York at 1-866-478-0556

Contents

Who Was Turner?

Joseph Mallord William Turner was a British landscape painter, watercolor artist, and printmaker. He is often known as "the painter of light" because of the brilliant colors he used in his **landscapes** and **seascapes**. He was born in 1775 at Maiden Lane, Covent Garden, in London, England.

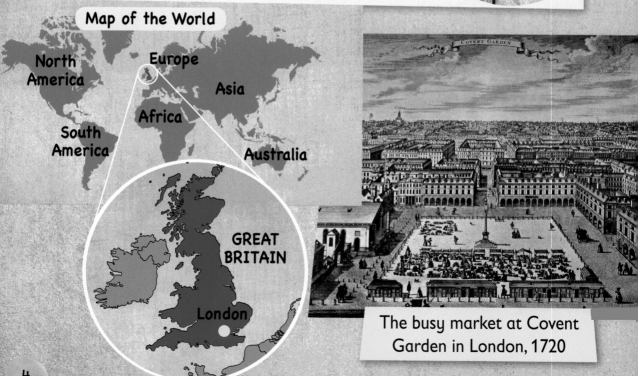

Map of the World

North America

Europe

Asia

Africa

South America

Australia

GREAT BRITAIN

London

The busy market at Covent Garden in London, 1720

Turner's father was a barber and wig maker. His mother was a butcher's daughter. Turner's younger sister died at age four, leaving him an only child. Turner's father encouraged his son's interest in art. He would display his son's artwork in the window of his barber's shop!

Staying with Family

When he was ten, Turner went to stay with his uncle. Turner colored in prints of landscapes while he was there. He became interested in art. A year later he visited Margate, a country town east of London. He did drawings of the buildings and countryside. Whenever he stayed with his uncle, Turner would fill a sketchbook with drawings and watercolors.

A watercolor of St. John's Church, Margate, painted when Turner was around 12 years old

Learning His Trade

Covent Garden was a busy area of London. Many people passed by his father's barber shop and saw Turner's paintings. At 12 years old, Turner was making money coloring prints. He started working with the artist and **engraver** Thomas Malton, drawing buildings and maps.

A View of the Archbishop's Palace, Lambeth.
This watercolor went in the Royal Academy's exhibition when Turner was just 15 years old!

A member of the Royal Academy of Arts noticed his paintings while having his hair cut. He was impressed with Turner's work and introduced him to the Royal Academy art school. Turner was accepted at the school when he was 15 years old.

The First Oil

Turner's watercolors hung at the school's famous exhibitions every year. In 1796, Turner had his first oil painting, *Fishermen at Sea*, below, accepted by the Royal Academy.

Prints Make Money

Turner earned money to help pay for his tuition by drawing engravings. He did designs for magazines. He also made copies of unfinished drawings by other artists. Their work inspired Turner and his **etchings** got better and better.

Neath, 1795. This drawing by Turner was published in the *Lady's Pocket Magazine.*

Turner began to travel to find inspiration for his pictures. A war in Europe meant that he traveled in Britain at first. He made his first trip to continental Europe in 1802, during a gap in the war with France. Switzerland's mountains and lakes inspired him.

Lake Thun

Turner visited Lake Thun in the Swiss Alps on his first tour in 1802. He made many pencil sketches of the lake in a sketchbook. Turner later did a watercolor of the same scene. Can you spot any changes to the figures in the painting below?

Becoming Successful

Turner's growing popularity led him to open a gallery at his new home in London. Turner exhibited watercolors done from drawings from his European tour.

The new gallery was a much better space than the crowded Academy gallery. It attracted some new customers. Walter Fawkes became a collector of his work, and became a close friend. Turner often stayed at his home, Farnley Hall.

Chamonix and Mont Blanc from the Path to the Montenvers, 1802. Many of Turner's paintings have faded over time. This painting would have had a blue sky and much greener trees.

No Money in the Bank

Even though Turner was earning a good deal of money, he never had a bank account. Turner bought houses and **shares** in companies with his money instead.

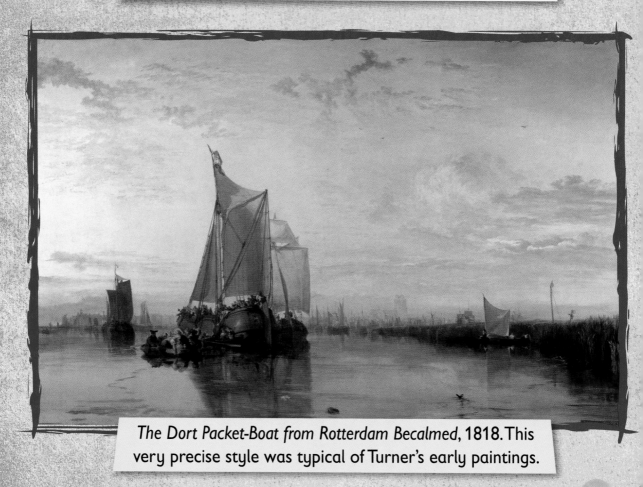

The Dort Packet-Boat from Rotterdam Becalmed, 1818. This very precise style was typical of Turner's early paintings.

Years with Two Halves

Turner would travel and sketch in the summer. When he was back in his studio in the winter he would use the sketches to help him create his paintings.

House Guest

Turner often stayed at friends' houses to paint. Turner had some wealthy friends! He stayed at the Earl of Egremont's estate, Petworth House.

Petworth, Sussex, the Seat of the Earl of Egremont: Dewy Morning, 1810

Turner's mother became mentally ill after the death of her daughter. She went to live in a hospital, and Turner's father came to live with him. He worked as Turner's assistant and helped to sell his paintings.

Keelmen Heaving in Coals by Moonlight, 1835

Painting the Weather

Turner liked to paint the effects of weather. *Calais Pier*, below, was created after Turner had taken his first trip abroad to Calais, France. The sea was very rough. The dark sailboat full of people in the center would have been his ferry. The painting was criticized. People thought it looked unfinished!

Calais Pier, 1803

Snow Storm—Steam-Boat off a Harbor's Mouth, 1842

Experiencing the Storm

Turner went to great lengths to get the right emotions into this painting, called *Snow Storm—Steam-Boat off a Harbor's Mouth*. Turner asked to be tied to a ship's mast during a storm, so that he could experience what it was like! The painting really gives you the feeling of what it would be like in a storm at sea. You wouldn't be able to see very much detail!

The Fighting Temeraire

Turner's most famous painting is probably *The Fighting Temeraire*. Painted in 1839, it shows a famous warship's last journey to the junkyard.

The Warship

The ship, the *HMS Temeraire*, was used during a great sea battle against France and Spain. The ship was the Royal Navy's most famous warship. Turner kept the painting in his studio and refused to sell it.

Turner lived during the **industrial revolution**. This was a time when many new things were invented. The steamship was taking over from ships with sails. In this picture the new little steam-driven tugboat represents the future. The old sailing ship represents the past. Most people don't think it is a sad painting, though. The new tough little tugboat is a sign that there will be a powerful, exciting future.

The painting's full title is *The Fighting Temeraire tugged to her last Berth to be broken up.*

Painting Trains

When Turner was born, people traveled by stagecoach. During his lifetime, the new railroads changed transportation forever. In the 1840s a train moving at around 60 miles per hour (96.5 km/h) was an amazing sight.

Turner began to use oil paint more like watercolor, using **transparent** washes of color. He liked painting light and movement. The painting *Rain, Steam, and Speed* is a good example of this **technique**. The train and bridges are hard to make out. This is not a painting of a train, but a painting of the effect of a train.

Rain, Steam, and Speed. The Great Western Railway, 1844.
Can you see the jackrabbit on the bridge ahead of the train?

Painter of Light

Turner painted this picture of Rome ten years after his last trip to the city. It was painted at the height of his career from sketches made on his two visits to the city. The light from a warm Italian late afternoon seems to shimmer in the picture.

Moon and Sun

When this painting was first shown at the Royal Academy, Turner put a line from a poem by Lord Byron next to it. "The moon is up, and yet it is not night, The sun as yet divides the day with her." Turner wanted the light effects of the sunset and the moon in his painting. The orb in the center is the moon.

Modern Rome–Campo Vaccino, 1839.
In 2010 this painting was sold for a record amount for a Turner picture. The Getty Museum in Los Angeles paid $44.9 million for the work!

Turner and Venice

Turner made many visits to Venice, Italy. Venice is famous for its canals. The buildings seem to float on the water. The sun reflects off the water with a shimmering light. The city inspired Turner to create some of his best paintings.

The Grand Canal, Venice, 1835

The Dogana and Santa Maria della Salute, Venice, 1843

With its water, weather, and light, Venice was the perfect place for Turner to paint. His buildings were not that accurate, though. The tower in *The Grand Canal* painting is much taller than it really is. What is accurate is the atmosphere and light.

A Romantic

Turner was a Romantic painter. Romantic painters use imagination, emotion, and expression in their work. In his paintings of Venice, Turner did not just record how the city looked, but added his own romantic impression of it.

Sunsets and Disasters

A little like a modern news photographer, Turner recorded disasters such as fires and shipwrecks in his work. Turner himself watched the burning of London's Houses of Parliament as it happened. He made sketches using pencil and watercolor from different places, including from a rented boat!

The Burning of the Houses of Parliament, 1835.
Turner painted the drama, flames, and smoke.
People watched from the riverbank and boats.

The Evening of the Deluge, 1843. Turner painted the bible story of Noah and the flood. You can see the rain approaching as Noah and his wife lie in their tent.

Volcanoes and Sunsets

In 1816, a huge volcano **erupted** in Indonesia. The ash in the air led to spectacular sunsets for years afterward. These sunsets inspired much of Turner's work.

Mount Tambora, Indonesia.

A Matter of Taste

Some critics thought Turner's paintings were too pale, or lacked detail. Turner's **personality** did not always make him friends, either. He could be quite rude. He had a strong London accent, and was described as looking a little like a farmer! Some people in the art world disliked him because of it.

His house and gallery fell into ruin. Visitors described it as having grimy windows and leaks in the roof. If it rained, visitors apparently needed an umbrella while they looked around!

Secret Life

For many years Turner lived with a woman, Sophia Booth, in a house by the river. He called himself Admiral Booth. Everyone thought that they were married, and that he was a seaman! No one knew he was the famous J.M.W. Turner!

Staffa, Fingal's Cave, 1832

The American collector James Lenox wanted to own a Turner painting. But he bought one without having seen it first! Lenox's friend chose *Staffa, Fingal's Cave* for him. Lenox had only seen Turner's etchings before. His friend was worried he may not like the painting. He was right! Lenox said the painting was **indistinct**. Turner replied "indistinctness is my **forte**!"

A Royal Academy Legacy

Turner exhibited for the last time at the Royal Academy in 1850. He was always a strong supporter of the Academy and always enjoyed "Varnishing Day." This was the day before the exhibition opened, when the artists could meet, and make finishing touches to their work.

The Red Buoy

Rival artist John Constable's colorful painting hung next to Turner's paler painting, *Helvoetsluys*, on Varnishing Day. Worried, Turner added a red buoy to his own **canvas**. This bright red mark completely took attention away from Constable's painting!

Turner on Varnishing Day, William Parrot, 1846. Turner would add last minute touches to his paintings.

Helvoetsluys, 1832. Note the red buoy in the sea's foreground.

Turner died in 1851 at age 76. His last words were said to be "The Sun is God." He was buried in St. Paul's Cathedral, London. Turner influenced the **Impressionist** and **Postimpressionist** painters that came after him. He is believed to be the greatest British landscape painter. Turner left a large amount of money to the Royal Academy to help struggling artists. He also left hundreds of paintings and drawings to the British nation.

Glossary

canvas (KAN-ves)
A piece of cloth used as a surface for painting.

engraver (en-GRAY-vur)
Someone who cuts or carves letters or designs.

erupted (ih-RUP-ted)
Exploded.

etchings (EH-chingz)
Prints made from an etched metal plate.

forte (FOR-tay)
The thing a person does very well; a strong point.

Impressionist (im-PREH-shuh-nist)
An artist who concentrates on the impression of a scene using unmixed primary colors and small brush strokes to simulate light.

indistinct (ihn-dih-STINCT)
Not distinct or clear.

industrial revolution (in-DUS-tree-ul reh-vuh-LOO-shun)
A period during which power-driven machinery was introduced.

landscapes
(LAND-skaypz)
Pictures of the
natural scenery.

personality
(per-suh-NA-lih-tee)
The emotions and
behavior that make a
person different.

Postimpressionist
(POHST-im-PREH-shuh-nist)
An artist who reacted
against the naturalism of
the Impressionists.

seascapes (SEE-skaypz)
Pictures of a scene at sea.

shares (SHAYRZ)
Equal portions of a
business that people own.

technique
(tek-NEEK)
A method of achieving a
desired aim.

transparent
(tranz-PAYR-ent)
Able to be seen through.

Websites

For web resources related to the
subject of this book, go to:
www.windmillbooks.com/weblinks
and select this book's title.

Read More

Civardi, Anne. *Action!* Movement in Art (Artventure). London: Wayland, 2005.

Kramer, Ann. *Artists*. Great Britons. London: Franklin Watts, 2007.

Thomson, Leo. *Place and Space*. Landscapes in Art (Artventure). London: Wayland, 2005.

Index